GETTYSBURG

James Bow

Crabtree Publishing Company

www.crabtreebooks.com

Crabtree Publishing Company
www.crabtreebooks.com

Author: James Bow
Publishing plan research and development:
   Sean Charlebois, Reagan Miller
   Crabtree Publishing Company
Photo research: Steve White-Thomson
Editors: Sonya Newland, Kathy Middleton
Design: Clare Nicholas/Tim Mayer
   (Mayer Media)
Cover design: Margaret Amy Salter
**Production coordinator and prepress
   technician:** Samara Parent
Print coordinator: Katherine Berti

Produced for Crabtree Publishing by
White-Thomson Publishing

Reading levels determined by
Publishing Solutions Group.
Content level: R
Readability level: M

Photographs:
Alamy: Classic Image: p. 31; © Look and
Learn/The Bridgeman Art Library: front
cover; Corbis: pp. 28–29; Bettmann: pp. 6–7,
12, 20–21; Dreamstime: Jk3291: pp. 44–45;
Getty Images: pp. 34–35; Library of Congress:
pp. 3, 8–9, 12–13, 29, 32–33, 39, 41; Mary
Evans Picture Library: p. 25; National Park
Service/ Gettysburg National Military Park:
p. 33; Bradley Schmehl: pp. 1, 4–5, 10–11,
16–17, 18–19, 22–23, 36–37, 40, 42–43;
Shutterstock: Caitlin Mirra: p. 45; Topfoto:
The Granger Collection: pp. 14–15, 38;
Thinkstock: back cover; U.S. National Guard:
H. Charles McBarron: pp. 26–27; Wikipedia:
p. 9; NARA: p. 20.

Library and Archives Canada Cataloguing in Publication

Bow, James, 1972-
   Gettysburg / James Bow.

(Crabtree chrome)
Includes index.
Issued also in electronic formats.
ISBN 978-0-7787-7928-5 (bound).--ISBN 978-0-7787-7937-7
(pbk.)

   1. Gettysburg, Battle of, Gettysburg, Pa., 1863--Juvenile
literature. I. Title. II. Series: Crabtree chrome

E475.53.B69 2012   j973.7'349   C2012-906750-4

Library of Congress Cataloging-in-Publication Data

Bow, James.
   Gettysburg / James Bow.
      p. cm. -- (Crabtree chrome)
   Includes index.
   ISBN 978-0-7787-7928-5 (reinforced library binding) --
ISBN 978-0-7787-7937-7 (pbk.) -- ISBN 978-1-4271-7854-1
(electronic pdf) -- ISBN 978-1-4271-7969-2 (electronic html)
   1. Gettysburg, Battle of, Gettysburg, Pa., 1863--Juvenile
literature. I. Title.

E475.53.B84 2012
973.7'349--dc23
                                        2012040200

Crabtree Publishing Company
www.crabtreebooks.com   1-800-387-7650

Printed in the U.S.A./112012/FA20121012

Published in Canada
Crabtree Publishing
616 Welland Ave.
St. Catharines, ON
L2M 5V6

Published in the United States
Crabtree Publishing
PMB 59051
350 Fifth Avenue, 59th Floor
New York, New York 10118

Published in the United Kingdom
Crabtree Publishing
Maritime House
Basin Road North, Hove
BN41 1WR

Published in Australia
Crabtree Publishing
3 Charles Street
Coburg North
VIC 3058

Contents

North Against South

The War Between the States

In 1861, less than one hundred years after becoming a country, the United States of America became involved in a **civil war**. Called the "War Between the States," the northern states, called the "Union," fought the southern states, called the "Confederacy."

A Bitter Fight

Two years later, the two armies would clash at the bloodiest battle of the Civil War in Gettysburg, Pennsylvania. Both sides believed that this battle could win them the war. Instead, the fighting went on for two more years after Gettysburg.

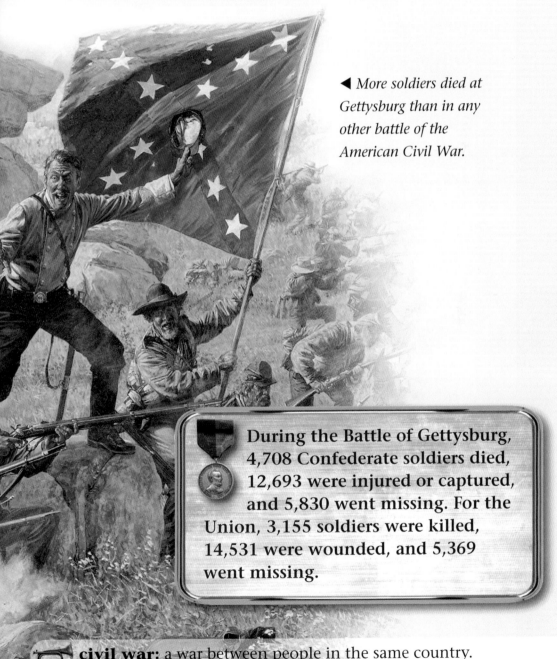

◀ *More soldiers died at Gettysburg than in any other battle of the American Civil War.*

During the Battle of Gettysburg, 4,708 Confederate soldiers died, 12,693 were injured or captured, and 5,830 went missing. For the Union, 3,155 soldiers were killed, 14,531 were wounded, and 5,369 went missing.

civil war: a war between people in the same country.

Different Ways of Life

Ways of life were very different in the northern
and southern states of the United States.
People in the South used **slaves** on their farms
and in their homes. In the North, people did
not agree with keeping slaves. The right to own
slaves and each state's right to decide for itself
about slavery became a dividing issue.

▼ *These slaves are working
on a cotton plantation in
Mississippi, in the southern
United States.*

The Election that Broke America

In 1860, Abraham Lincoln was elected president. Lincoln did not want to ban slavery, but he wanted to stop it from spreading to any more states. Many southerners saw this as an attack on their way of life. They also felt that the government should not interfere in the rights of states to decide whether they would be "slave states" or "free states."

▲ *When Lincoln became president, the southern states worried that he might eventually try to ban slavery in the South.*

"Our government is founded ... upon the truth that the Negro is not equal to the white man."

Alexander Stephens, vice-president of the Confederacy

slaves: people who have to work for someone without payment.

Leaving the Union

Angry at the new government, some southern states decided to leave the Union. South Carolina was the first state to leave. Soon, Mississippi, Florida, Alabama, Georgia, Louisiana, and Texas left, too. These "rebel" states joined together and called themselves the Confederate States of America.

▼ *This map shows the sides that the different states were on in the Civil War.*

BRITISH TERRITORIES

WASHINGTON TERRITORY

DAKOTA TERRITORY

MINNESOTA

VERMONT

MAINE

OREGON

WISCONSIN

MICHIGAN

NEW YORK

NEW HAMPSHIRE

MASSACHUSETTS

NEBRASKA TERRITORY

IOWA

PENNSYLVANIA

RHODE ISLAND

NEVADA TERRITORY

UTAH TERRITORY

COLORADO TERRITORY

KANSAS

ILLINOIS

INDIANA

OHIO

Gettysburg

WEST VIRGINIA

CONNECTICUT

NEW JERSEY

DELAWARE

CALIFORNIA

MISSOURI

KENTUCKY

VIRGINIA

MARYLAND

NEW MEXICO TERRITORY

INDIAN TERRITORY

ARKANSAS

TENNESSEE

NORTH CAROLINA

ATLANTIC OCEAN

PACIFIC OCEAN

MISSISSIPPI

ALABAMA

SOUTH CAROLINA

GEORGIA

N
W E
S

TEXAS

LOUISIANA

FLORIDA

◻ Free states
◻ Slave states that seceded before the Civil War began
◻ Slave states that seceded after the Civil War began
◻ Slave states that remained loyal to the Union
◻ Territories

Gulf of Mexico

MEXICO

0   500 miles
0   500 kilometres

The Shooting Starts

On April 12, 1861, the first shot of the Civil War was fired by South Carolina at a supply ship sent by the U.S. government to Fort Sumter. Soon after, the states of Virginia, Arkansas, Tennessee, and North Carolina joined the **Confederacy**.

◀ *The Civil War began when the Confederates opened fire on a Union ship at Fort Sumter in South Carolina.*

The Civil War turned friends, neighbors, and even families against each other. During a battle in 1862, a Confederate captain, William Goldsborough, took his own brother prisoner. Charles Goldsborough had been fighting for the Union.

Confederacy: a group of states.

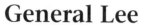

General Lee

Robert E. Lee was an officer in the United States Army when the war broke out. Lincoln asked Lee to lead the Union army. But Lee was a loyal southerner. He did not want to fight against his home state of Virginia. Instead he became the leader of the Confederate Army of Northern Virginia.

▶ Lee (in the middle of this picture) did not like slavery and he thought the South should stay in the Union, but he fought for the Confederates anyway.

The War Drags On

During 1862, the war began to go badly for the Union. Lee won some important battles. People in the North were shocked and afraid. They had more soldiers and more weapons than the South. They had thought they would crush the Confederacy in just a few months. But the war dragged on.

"How can I draw my sword upon Virginia, my **native** state?"

General Robert E. Lee

native: the place where you are born.

The Emancipation Proclamation

On January 1, 1863, President Lincoln issued the Emancipation Proclamation. The Proclamation declared that all the slaves in the "rebel" states were free. This was just what the South had been afraid of. Confederate soldiers fought even harder to defend their land and their way of life.

▲ *This picture shows Abraham Lincoln (third from the left) reading the Emancipation Proclamation with members of his government.*

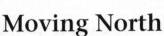

Moving North

By winning battles, Lee thought he could force Lincoln to make a deal with the South to stop the war. By 1863, Lee's plan was working. Lincoln feared the Union was close to losing. Up till now, most battles had been fought in southern states. Lee decided it was time to bring the war to the North.

"My **paramount** objective in this struggle is to save the Union ... If I could save the Union without freeing any slaves then I would do it, and if I could save it by freeing all the slaves I would do it."

President Abraham Lincoln

▼ *The Emancipation Proclamation allowed African-Americans to join the army and fight for the Union.*

paramount: most important.

Lee Marches On

In May 1863, Lee won a key battle at Chancellorsville in Virginia. Afterward, he marched his army into the northern state of Pennsylvania. After the loss at Chancellorsville, President Lincoln knew he had to replace the **commander** of the Union army. He chose General George Meade and ordered Meade to stop Lee from moving north.

▼ *At Chancellorsville, Lee beat the Union army even though he had half the number of soldiers.*

Old Soldiers

The two commanders, Lee and Meade, knew each other well. They were both older soldiers. They had both been educated at the military college of West Point and served together in an earlier war. Lee knew that Meade would be hard to beat.

> There is a story that at the end of the war Lee and Meade met each other as friends again. Lee asked Meade, "What are you doing with all that gray in your beard?" Meade replied, "You have to answer for most of it!"

commander: a leader.

The Battle Begins

Gettysburg Before the Battle

Gettysburg was a market town in Pennsylvania. About 2,400 people lived there. Many of them were shoemakers or worked in the town's **tanneries**. There was also an important carriage-making industry in Gettysburg. More people lived and worked on farms in the surrounding area. It was a busy and thriving town.

Searching for Supplies

Lincoln sent Meade to Pennsylvania to drive Lee out of the North. As Meade hurried to organize his army near Gettysburg, the first Confederate troops arrived. Running low on supplies, the barefoot Confederate soldiers had been sent ahead to search Gettysburg for boots and other supplies. In the distance they saw Union soldiers marching toward them.

▼ *The Confederates arrived in Gettysburg in late June. They saw the Union army coming, and began preparing for battle.*

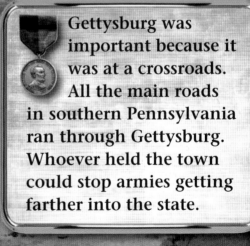

Gettysburg was important because it was at a crossroads. All the main roads in southern Pennsylvania ran through Gettysburg. Whoever held the town could stop armies getting farther into the state.

tanneries: places where animal skins are turned into leather.

McPherson Ridge

The Confederates were surprised to see the Union forces already there, and the two armies immediately began to fight. Union troops took up positions along McPherson Ridge. This was a stretch of high ground to the west of the town. Then more than 3,000 Confederate soldiers arrived.

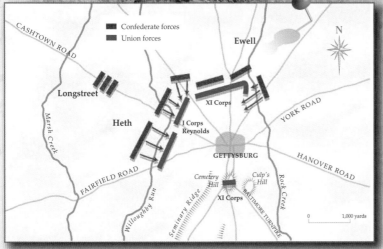

◀ *This map shows the positions of the Union and Confederate soldiers on the first day of the Battle of Gettysburg, July 1, 1863.*

Attack!

At first, there were many more Confederate soldiers than Union soldiers. The Union troops fought hard. Against great odds, they held off the Confederates until **reinforcements** arrived, led by John Reynolds. No sooner had Reynolds ordered his men to fight than he was shot and killed. His death caused confusion and delay in the fight.

▲ *Union leader John Reynolds was called by many the best general in the army. He was killed at the start of the battle.*

Spencer carbine guns helped Union troops in this first fight at Gettysburg. These guns could load and fire faster than the guns that the Confederate soldiers had.

reinforcements: new soldiers sent to help in a battle.

Lee Arrives

General Lee arrived later that afternoon. He was shocked to see that the Union soldiers were holding off his own troops. Lee's **scout**, Jeb Stuart, was off fighting elsewhere and could not gather reports for the general. Without reports, Lee did not know what he was up against.

▲ Jeb Stuart was leader of the Confederate cavalry (soldiers on horses). The cavalry was separated from the rest of the Confederates at the start of the battle.

Lee Orders the Attack

Lee told his men to back off, so he could decide what to do next. Soon, Lee saw his chance. He ordered his troops to move round and attack the Union army from the side. The Union soldiers were driven back into the town.

▼ *Union soldiers retreated southward through the town as the Confederates attacked from the side.*

"You, sir, are the eyes of this army. Without you, we are blind. That has happened once. It must never happen again."

General Lee to Jeb Stuart

scout: someone who goes ahead of an army to report back.

Street Fighting

Confederate soldiers chased the Union troops into Gettysburg. Soon, hundreds of soldiers were fighting in the streets. The townspeople fled to their houses to escape the battle going on outside. Many Union soldiers were captured or killed. The Confederates had the Union army on the run!

▼ *The Confederates (in gray) fought hand to hand with Union soldiers (in blue) in the streets of Gettysburg.*

Taking the High Ground

Union commanders ordered soldiers to **retreat** toward a spot called Cemetery Hill. General Lee knew if they made it to this high ground, it would be hard for his Confederate forces to attack them. Lee wanted to take Cemetery Hill first. But his order was ignored. Union soldiers were able to regroup on Culp's Hill and Cemetery Hill.

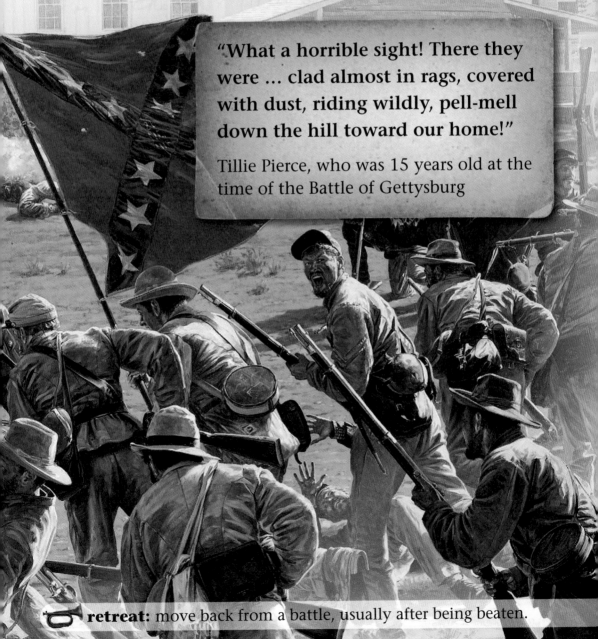

"What a horrible sight! There they were … clad almost in rags, covered with dust, riding wildly, pell-mell down the hill toward our home!"

Tillie Pierce, who was 15 years old at the time of the Battle of Gettysburg

retreat: move back from a battle, usually after being beaten.

Stalemate

The Union Digs In

By the second day, reinforcements had arrived on both sides. Lee wanted to attack Cemetery Hill, but the Union had already built **defenses** there. General James Longstreet had a better plan. South of Cemetery Hill was a hill called Little Round Top. It was undefended. Confederate troops could attack from there.

▼ *By the second day of the battle, Union troops held the high ground—the ridges and hills around Gettysburg.*

▶ *General Meade ordered his men to prepare to defend their position on the high ground.*

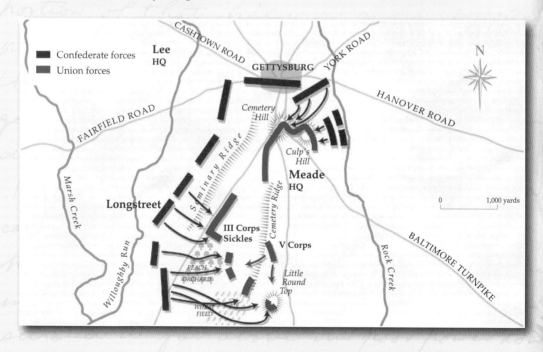

Help from the Townspeople

Boys from the town of Gettysburg were excited to see the war up close. They visited the Union camps and brought bread to the hungry soldiers. The boys would take the horses to watering troughs so they could drink. Other townspeople helped by looking after Union soldiers who had been wounded.

"I noticed a great deal of confusion, soldiers riding both ways ... and as soon as I got up to the camp, I dismounted, gave the loaf of bread to the soldier who tore out a piece of the bread, jumped on his horse, and fell into line."

Hugh Ziegler, a 10-year-old boy from Gettysburg

defenses: things that protect an area when it is under attack.

Professor Chamberlain

General Meade, however, also realized that Little Round Top was undefended. He ordered Colonel Joshua Chamberlain and his men, the 20th Maine, to take the hill for the Union army. Before the war Chamberlain had been a college professor. He had never fought before, but he turned out to be a great army leader.

▲ *The men of the 20th Maine charged downhill and scattered the Confederate soldiers.*

The Fight for Little Round Top

The 20th Maine did not have much ammunition left. Despite this, they fought the Confederates bravely. Chamberlain ordered his men to charge at the enemy with their **bayonets**. The Confederate soldiers did not realize the 20th Maine could not fire their guns. They ran away from the attack. Chamberlain won Little Round Top.

Soldier: Colonel! I've been moving these Rebs [rebels] with an empty musket!
Chamberlain: Not so loud!

bayonets: blades fixed to the front of a gun, used for stabbing.

27

The Valley of Death

Lee could not wait any longer. He had to attack.
Confederate soldiers marched up toward Cemetery
Hill under a hail of fire from the Union guns. From
the high position, it was easy for the Union army to
stop the Confederate advance. So many men died
that the area became known as the Valley of Death.

▼ *By the end of the second day, the*
Confederate army had gained only a little
ground, and the Union still held Cemetery Hill.

Fighting in the Dark

As night fell, both sides found it hard to see in the dark. Some men shot soldiers on their own side by accident. Commanders ordered the fighting to stop. Already over 30,000 men had been killed or **wounded** at Gettysburg. This was more than any other battle so far in the Civil War.

"My dead and wounded were nearly as great in number as those still on duty. They literally covered the ground."

Confederate Colonel William Oates

▼ *These Confederate soldiers were killed during the attack on Cemetery Hill.*

wounded: hurt in battle.

The Turning Point

Fresh Troops Arrive

By the third day at Gettysburg both sides were exhausted. But they knew the battle was not over yet. New troops had arrived for both sides, and this gave the tired soldiers hope. A Confederate **division** led by General George Pickett came from the west.

▼ *This map shows the positions of the Union and Confederate troops during the third day of the Battle of Gettysburg.*

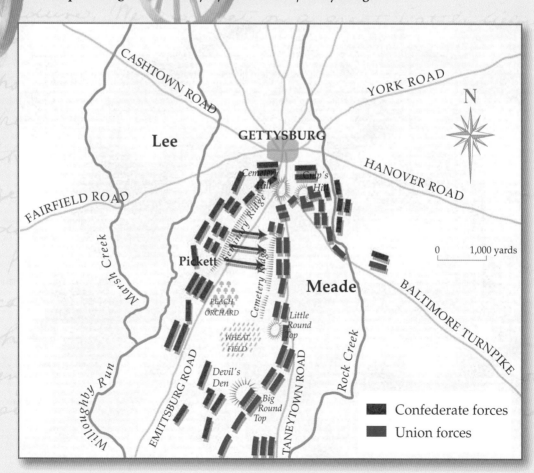

CASHTOWN ROAD

YORK ROAD

N

Lee

GETTYSBURG

Cemetery Hill

Culp's Hill

HANOVER ROAD

FAIRFIELD ROAD

Marsh Creek

Pickett

Seminary Ridge

Cemetery Ridge

Meade

PEACH ORCHARD

Little Round Top

WHEAT FIELD

Devil's Den

Big Round Top

EMMITSBURG ROAD

Willoughby Run

TANEYTOWN ROAD

Rock Creek

BALTIMORE TURNPIKE

0   1,000 yards

◼ Confederate forces

◼ Union forces

Final Attack

When the fresh troops were ready, Lee ordered a final attack on Cemetery Hill. Pickett was chosen to lead the charge. Once again, Longstreet told Lee that attacking Cemetery Hill was the wrong move. This time, Lee did not listen to him. It would be a costly mistake.

▼ *Longstreet did not agree with Lee's plan to attack Cemetery Hill, but he had to obey his leader. Here, Longstreet (left) gives General Pickett his orders.*

Longstreet was second in command to Lee, and Lee called him "my old war horse." Although Longstreet was a great army commander, Lee ignored his advice during the Battle of Gettysburg.

division: a large group of soldiers.

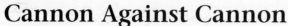

Cannon Against Cannon

To weaken the Union's defenses, Lee ordered cannons to fire at the Union lines before they attacked them. Union forces fired back with cannons of their own. But Confederate cannons were aimed too high and did little damage. Union forces stopped their cannon fire to save **artillery** and make the enemy think they had been beaten.

▲ *The Battle of Gettysburg was the first time that so many cannons were used in an attack.*

Pickett's Charge

Finally, Lee ordered the charge. Then the Union army switched from cannonballs to canisters. These weapons burst apart when fired from a cannon. Thousands of iron balls sprayed across the battlefield. Hundreds of Confederate soldiers were killed instantly.

▲ *As Lee ordered the charge, more than 12,000 Confederate soldiers ran forward, shouting and firing.*

"The moans of my wounded boys, the sight of the dead, upturned faces flood my soul with grief."

George Pickett, in a letter to his wife just after the Battle of Gettysburg

artillery: big guns like cannons, able to fire great distances.

Holding Fire

The Confederate soldiers kept moving forward. The Union soldiers waited under cover on the high ground. When the Confederates were close enough, Union soldiers began firing with their muskets from the safety of their trenches. Confederate troops were **massacred**. The North had won the hard-fought Battle of Gettysburg.

The Legend of Pickett's Charge

Soldiers who survived Pickett's Charge realized they had taken part in a key moment in the Civil War. Some Union soldiers wrote about how brave their Confederate enemy had been, charging toward almost certain death.

▼ *Pickett's Charge became one of the most famous battles in history.*

"I recognized then and there that this battle was to be, in all probability, regarded as a great turning point in history."

Levi Baker, a Union soldier on Cemetery Hill during Pickett's Charge

massacred: when many people are killed at the same time.

The Battle Ends

Even after Pickett's disastrous charge, Lee kept fighting.
The Confederate **colors** flew briefly above Cemetery Hill,
but the soldiers who raised the flag were quickly killed
or captured. The Union army still held the high ground.
Lee knew Meade had won and ordered a retreat.

▲ *After Pickett's Charge, the
Confederate army left Gettysburg.
One Confederate officer said:
"We gained nothing but glory,
and lost our bravest men."*

Too Tired to Go On

Meade wanted to chase Lee and wipe out the remains of the Confederate army. If he had done this, he could have ended the Civil War there and then. But Meade knew his army was too tired to carry on fighting right away. So the Confederates escaped.

> "I am very—very—grateful to you for the magnificent success you gave the cause of the country at Gettysburg."
>
> Abraham Lincoln in a letter to General George Meade

colors: a military flag showing which army is in control.

After Gettysburg

What Happened Next?

The Confederacy had lost badly at Gettysburg. The **"invincible"** Lee had been beaten. The news hurt morale in the South. It gave the North encouragement to fight on. This turning point battle would help President Lincoln win the next election. The North would make no deal to end the war.

▲ *General Lee surrenders to the Union army in April 1865.*

The Beginning of the End

From this point on, the Civil War was fought only in the southern states. The Union army began a determined attack. Union soldiers marched through the South, fighting fiercely and taking over southern towns and cities. Finally, in April 1865, the Confederacy surrendered.

Dealing with the bodies at Gettysburg was a huge task. Elizabeth Thorn was the wife of the cemetery keeper in the town. She dug over 100 graves herself in the summer heat.

▼ *After the armies left Gettysburg, the townspeople began burying the dead.*

invincible: someone who cannot be beaten.

The Gettysburg Address

In 1863, while the war was still raging, President Lincoln was invited to open a cemetery at Gettysburg for the soldiers who had died there. The president gave a speech that became known as the Gettysburg Address. He thanked the soldiers and promised that the country they had fought for would not be broken apart.

▼ *Union soldiers kneel in prayer at Gettysburg.*

The Idea of America

Lincoln had not wanted to drag the United States into war. He felt that it was the only way to save the country. In his speech, Lincoln talked about **equality** and freedom. He said that these ideas were what America had been built on. They are still important to Americans today.

"That we here highly resolve these dead shall not have died in vain; that the nation shall have a new birth of freedom, and that government of the people by the people for the people, shall not perish from the earth."

President Lincoln's Gettysburg Address

▼ *President Lincoln delivering the Gettysburg Address.*

equality: when things are fair for all people.

The Unknown Soldier

After the battle, the body of a Union soldier was found alone a little way from the battlefield. He held in his hands a photograph of three children. This touched the hearts of the American people. They tried to find out who this unknown soldier was. Eventually they found out that his name was Amos Humiston.

▼ *Soldiers killed on the battlefield were often buried in shallow graves where they died.*

Each year, thousands of people re-enact Civil War battles. They do this to honor the men who took part and remember those who died.

The Great Reunion

July 1, 1913, marked 50 years since the Battle of Gettysburg. The state of Pennsylvania organized a **reunion** to remember the battle. Over 50,000 Civil War soldiers went back to Gettysburg. There was no anger between soldiers from the two sides any more. Old enemies ate together as friends, and put the past behind them.

reunion: when people meet again after a long time apart.

Gettysburg Today

Gettysburg was the bloodiest battle fought in the United States. Today, the Gettysburg National Park remembers the soldiers who fought and died. The National Parks Service keeps the fields as they were in 1863.

▼ *People honor the soldiers who died in the Civil War by re-enacting the famous battles such as Gettysburg.*

The Fields Where They Died

The park has over 1,400 **monuments** and three historic houses. More than 400 cannons have been left in place. There is a museum about the battle and the Civil War. Thousands of people visit the park every year, to remember the Battle of Gettysburg.

▲ *This statue of General George Meade is one of many monuments in the Gettysburg National Park.*

"Honor to the Soldier, and Sailor everywhere, who bravely bears his country's cause."

Abraham Lincoln

 monuments: things built to honor the dead.

45

Learning More

Books

The Battle of Gettysburg:
Would You Lead the Fight?
by Elaine Landau
(Enslow Elementary, 2009)

What Was the Battle
of Gettysburg?
by Jim O'Connor, James
Bennett, and John Mantha
(Grosset & Dunlap, 2012)

Gettysburg
by Josh Gregory
(Scholastic, 2011)

Bull Run to Gettysburg:
Early Battles of the Civil War
by Don Nardo
(Compass Point Books, 2011)

Websites

http://www.nps.gov/gett/forkids/
index.htm
PBS Kids: Gettysburg National
Military Park

http://www.ducksters.com/history/
civil_war.php
The American Civil War for
Kids

http://thisweekinthecivilwar.com/
This Week in the Civil War

http://www.historynet.com/civil-
war-times
Civil War Times

Glossary

artillery Big guns like cannons, able to fire great distances

bayonets Blades fixed to the front of a gun, used for stabbing

civil war A war between people in the same country

colors A military flag showing which army is in control

commander A leader

Confederacy A group of states

defenses Things that protect an area when it is under attack

division A large group of soldiers

equality When things are fair for all people

invincible Someone who cannot be beaten

massacred When many people are killed at the same time

monuments Things built to honor the dead

native The place where you are born

paramount Most important

reinforcements New soldiers sent to help in a battle

retreat Move back from a battle, usually after being beaten

reunion When people meet again after a long time apart

scout Someone who goes ahead of an army to report back

slaves People who have to work for someone without payment

tanneries Places where animal skins are turned into leather

wounded Hurt in battle

Index

Entries in **bold** refer to pictures